# ACTION EVENTS

# SUPER CROSS

## MOTORCYCLE RACING

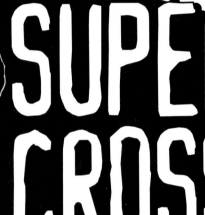

**ACTION EVENTS**

# SUPER CROSS
## MOTORCYCLE RACING

By Jeff Savage

**CRESTWOOD HOUSE**
Parsippany, New Jersey

Photo Credits
(all photos) SRO Motorsports
Cover and book design by Liz Kril
Copyright ©1997 by Silver Burdett Press

Published by Crestwood House,
A Division of Simon & Schuster,
299 Jefferson Road, Parsippany, NJ 07054

First Edition
Printed in the United States of America
10 9  8 7 6 5 4 3 2  1

**Library of Congress Cataloging-in-Publication Data**
Savage, Jeff, 1961-
    Supercross motorcycle racing/by Jeff Savage.—1st ed.
          p. cm.—(Action events)
    Includes index.
    Summary: Covers the history, vehicles, techniques, famous participants, and important events in the relatively new sport of supercross racing.
    ISBN 0-89686-887-7 (lib. bdg.)—ISBN 0-382-39292-2 (pbk.)
    1. Motocross—Juvenile literature. 2. Motorcycle racing—Juvenile literature. [1. Motocross. 2. Motorcycle racing.]
I. Title. II. Series
GV1060. 12.S38  1997
796.7′56—dc20                                  95–32758

# CONTENTS

# CHAPTER 1

# A CHAMPION RACER

Something was wrong with Jeremy McGrath. He was sluggish, passive. It was as though he didn't care about winning.

The place was Jack Murphy Stadium in San Diego, California, and Jeremy was riding his red 250**cc** Honda. But that was the only thing the fans recognized about the boy wonder of indoor motorcycle racing.

Jeremy had won the first three events of the 1994 American Motorcyclist Association (AMA) Supercross series. Eighty miles to the north in Anaheim, a week earlier, the twenty-two-year-old sensation had won by a whopping 20 seconds. And Jeremy was coming off his rookie season of 1993, in which he won a record ten **supercross** events. He was the new king of supercross. So why did he look so lazy in San Diego in a **heat race**?

It turned out that Jeremy had the flu. He hadn't eaten solid food for two days. He barely had enough strength to stay on his motorcycle. He even crashed midway through the heat race with Mike Craig.

Somehow Jeremy qualified for the final, but just barely.

After Jeremy crossed the finish line, he rode directly to the tunnel where an ambulance was parked. He got off his bike and sagged to the ground.

Paramedics rushed over and quickly administered oxygen. They told Jeremy that he shouldn't compete in the

> JEREMY MCGRATH IS ONE OF THE GREATEST SUPERCROSS RACERS EVER.

20-lap final. Jeremy gasped for air and said, "I'm racing. I *have* to."

Jeremy, of course, did *not* have to race. But he *thought* he had to. Jeremy's inner drive is as great as that of any athlete in sports.

The final began in the cool night air, with Jeff Matiasevich taking the early lead. Mike Craig was right behind in second place. Jeremy was fifth. And he wasn't happy about it.

Mike passed Jeff on the second lap and Jeff never threatened again. Jeremy was determined to move up. Fifth place would be fine for most riders suffering from the flu—but not for Jeremy. Slowly, carefully, he inched his way closer to the lead riders. He passed Mike LaRocco to move into fourth place. Next he passed Doug Henry to move into third. Then he passed Brian Swink to take second place, right behind Mike Craig. His body ached from the flu, but he put his discomfort out of his mind.

Over the jumps and **whoop-de-doos** Jeremy flew, sometimes airborne as high as 30 feet. He battled through **hairpin turns**, then gunned the **throttle** down the **straightaway** at 70 miles an hour.

JEREMY CLEARS JUMPS AND WHOOP-DE-DOOS BETTER THAN ANY RIDER TODAY.

On lap 12 Jeremy made his move. He passed Mike on the inside. There was really nothing Mike could do. He had seen the back of the McGrath jersey many times before.

Mike Kiedrowski made a late push for Jeremy but couldn't catch him. Jeremy crossed the finish line first. Again! He had won his fourth straight national supercross event of 1994. Even the flu couldn't beat him!

# Chapter 2
# The Great Riders

There have been a number of distinguished champions since the start of supercross racing in 1972.

Many people believe the greatest rider of all time was Rick Johnson, who won 28 main events before an injury cut short his career. Rick had won the first five events of the 1989 AMA Supercross series when a serious wrist injury forced him to retire.

Right behind Rick in the all-time winners column is "Hurricane" Bob Hannah, who racked up 27 victories with his all-out, feet-off-the-footpegs style of racing. Bob had won three consecutive yearly titles between 1977 and 1979, when a water-skiing accident ended his racing career.

Then there's David Bailey, the stepson of one of the sport's pioneers, Gary Bailey. David's super-smooth riding style carried him to 12 victories, including the 1983 overall title. Unfortunately, David's career was cut short in 1987 by a horrible crash that left him paralyzed. He now competes in wheelchair races.

Other great riders of the past include slick Broc Glover, daring Donnie Hansen, hyperaggressive Mark Barnett, "Too Tall" Mike Bell, and Damon Bradshaw, who began racing motorcycles at age three and competed in his first motorcycle race at age four.

IT TAKES SKILL TO MANEUVER A BIKE IN TRAFFIC AND GAIN THE LEAD.

THERE HAVE BEEN MANY DISTINGUISHED SUPERCROSS CHAMPIONS SINCE THE SPORT BEGAN IN 1972.

Now we can add to this great list the name Jeremy McGrath. When Jeremy entered his third year of competition, in 1995, he already had Rick Johnson's all-time win record in his sights. "No question about it. Jeremy is the best rider today," says veteran rider Jeff Ward.

Most motorcycle racers begin competing at a very young age. Jeremy rode his first motorcycle at age six, but he didn't enter his first race until he was fourteen. He preferred riding **BMX bikes** with his friends. The advantage Jeremy had over most boys his age was a dirt track, with jumps, that his father built for him behind the house. "I taught myself," Jeremy says. "I came home from school and rode on my track until it got dark or I ran out of gas. Every day I was constantly building new jumps that were higher and farther apart. I learned how to jump, but I didn't have any style. Nor did I care about style. When I was twelve years old, all I wanted to do was jump high and far and go fast. At that time a career in **motocross** hadn't even entered my mind."

When Jeremy did begin to enter races at age fourteen, he discovered that he was among the best riders for his age. At sixteen, he was competing in national events. He won the 125cc Western Region Supercross Championship in 1991 and 1992. He then joined the bigger 250cc class in the AMA Supercross series and won a record ten events in 1993. No one could have predicted so much success—not even Jeremy.

"Actually, I surprised myself," he says. "When I got my first two wins, I was like 'Yeah, man, this is pretty neat, but can I keep doing it?' I kept doing it, and it became normal. After I won four in a row, I kind of expected it of myself."

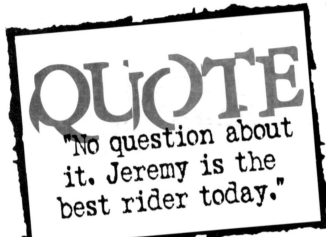

QUOTE

"No question about it. Jeremy is the best rider today."

There is a tremendous amount of pressure on supercross riders. Their families and friends expect them to win. Their sponsors expect them to win. Their fans expect them to win. One thing that separates Jeremy from other riders is his ability to handle this pressure.

"My biggest asset is that I can do what I'm doing at such a high-pressure job and not even worry about it," he says. "If someone puts pressure on me, it doesn't matter. I'm just having too much fun. I can't ride like I do if I'm not having fun. Making covers of magazines and

the riders who come in after a bad race—throwing things, cursing, and causing a scene. I just count my blessings every day that I'm where I'm at today, doing what I love."

Jeremy can also count plenty of cash in the bank. Supercross racing has made him quite wealthy at a young age. For instance, after winning the 1993 AMA title, Jeremy bought a boat, a house, a Chevy truck, and a BMX bike. "Sometimes I want to spend more money, but my parents talk me out of it," he says.

winning races is nice, but I'm doing this just for the fun. Most guys can't say that.

"I don't look at a bad race like everyone else. If I lose a race, I don't care. I can blow it off. I can't stand

# Chapter 3

# The Birth of Supercross Racing

The first motorcycle was invented back in 1885. It was nothing more than a bicycle with a motor attached under the seat. The words *motor* and *bicycle* were combined to make the word *motorcycle*.

Early motorcycles were heavy machines that moved slowly. But American companies—such as Harley-Davidson, Royal, and Indian—soon began making lighter, faster motorcycles because riders began racing them. Motorcycle races were held at county fairgrounds on oval-shaped racetracks for horses.

In the late 1940s, a new type of motorcycle race was created in Paris, France. It was staged on a closed course over natural, rough terrain.

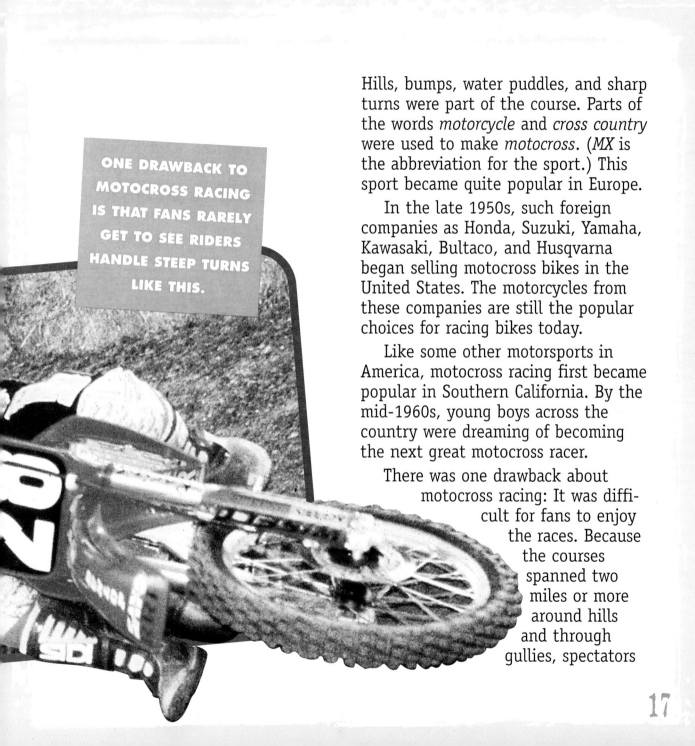

ONE DRAWBACK TO MOTOCROSS RACING IS THAT FANS RARELY GET TO SEE RIDERS HANDLE STEEP TURNS LIKE THIS.

Hills, bumps, water puddles, and sharp turns were part of the course. Parts of the words *motorcycle* and *cross country* were used to make *motocross*. (*MX* is the abbreviation for the sport.) This sport became quite popular in Europe.

In the late 1950s, such foreign companies as Honda, Suzuki, Yamaha, Kawasaki, Bultaco, and Husqvarna began selling motocross bikes in the United States. The motorcycles from these companies are still the popular choices for racing bikes today.

Like some other motorsports in America, motocross racing first became popular in Southern California. By the mid-1960s, young boys across the country were dreaming of becoming the next great motocross racer.

There was one drawback about motocross racing: It was difficult for fans to enjoy the races. Because the courses spanned two miles or more around hills and through gullies, spectators could not follow the action. The fans gathered near the finish, where every so often the riders would zoom past. But most often they could only *hear* the motorcycles out on the courses.

On March 11, 1972, this problem was solved. All the action was brought into plain sight on the infield of Daytona International Speedway at Daytona Beach, Florida, while fans watched from the comfort of their seats. Supercross was born.

In the decades since, supercross racing has blossomed into one of the most popular motorsports in the United States. The American Motorcyclist Association oversees the biggest series today, but thousands of other events are staged across the country as well.

Events are divided into classes, according to engine size. Engines are measured in cubic centimeters. The most popular classes are 125cc, 250cc, and 500cc. Regardless of engine size, all supercross motorcycles share two distinct characteristics: They have special suspension systems that cushion the ride over the grueling course, and they are extremely light.

QUOTE

"Supercross racing is one of the most popular motorsports in the United States."

Just how popular is the sport of supercross today? Racers on the AMA **circuit** are competing for more than $3 million in prize money and bonuses. Millions of Americans tune in to each of the 16 events televised by ESPN, a sports network. Also watching is a massive worldwide audience that includes Germany, Japan, Australia, England, and more than 70 other countries.

RIDERS COMPETE
FOR MILLIONS OF
DOLLARS IN PRIZE
MONEY AND
BONUSES.

# CHAPTER 4

Jimmy Weinert won the first supercross race in 1972 at Daytona International Speedway. But it wasn't until an event later that year that supercross was recognized around the world. It happened July 8 at the Los Angeles Memorial Coliseum. Motocross racing had started in France, and European riders, like Belgium's Roger DeCoster, still considered themselves to be superior to their American counterparts. Now riders in the United States were challenging the Europeans to a supercross race, and 35,000 fans turned out to see the competition.

The champion would be the racer who collected the most points in a three-race competition. In each of the races, first place was worth 10 points, second place was worth 9, third place was 8, and so on. It would take three good efforts to be the champion.

When it was all over, little-known Marty Tripes from Santee, California, had scored a surprising victory. Three riders from Sweden—Torlief Hansen, Arne Kring, and Haken Andersson—won the three individual races. But Marty

Tripes had finished second in all three events! He was clearly the most consistent racer. What's even more surprising is that Marty was just sixteen years old and this was his first competition ever!

The Los Angeles Coliseum was also the site of one of the most spectacular finishes in supercross history. A large crowd turned out on June 24, 1978, to see a prestigious group of twenty riders battle for the national points title.

Kawasaki rider Gary Semics led for most of the race, while Yamaha rider Mike Bell worked his way up from a mid-pack start. But all eyes were focused on the defending champ Hurricane Bob Hannah, who was fourteenth at the start. Bob passed rider after rider to reach fifth place but then crashed and dropped back to the middle of the pack. A few laps later, after Bob had worked his way back toward the lead, he was involved in a four-rider pileup. By now Mike Bell had moved into second place, behind Gary. Determined, Bob clawed his way toward the front again. With three laps left, Mike moved past Gary for the lead. But Bob was coming fast. Two laps from the finish, Bob passed Gary to take over second place and was closing in on Mike, who had never won before. On the last lap, Bob stuck his front wheel next to Mike's but couldn't get past him. Mike held on at the finish lap to win his first event in one of the sport's most exciting races.

**THERE HAVE BEEN SOME AWESOME RACES THROUGHOUT SUPERCROSS HISTORY.**

Another memorable race took place on March 5, 1983, in Atlanta's Fulton County Stadium, where a terrific rainstorm had turned the dirt track into a giant mud bog. David Bailey was in the lead midway through the race when he went airborne over a jump. "There were two big ruts on both sides of the jump," David remembers, "and the middle one hardly seemed used. I hit it and got stuck instantly. I guess that's why nobody was using it." David's motorcycle was stuck in the muck, and he couldn't pull it out. One by one, the other riders went flying past. Soon, however, some of them became stuck as well. Mark Barnett assumed the lead. By now the riders were caked with mud, and it was impossible to identify them. Mark went on to win by 45 seconds. Long after the fans had filed out of the stadium, some of the riders were still trying to pull their cycles from the mud.

David Bailey's most memorable race came three years later, on a cold winter night in Southern California. It was January 18, 1986, and the opening round of the AMA Supercross series. Over 70,000 fans were jammed into Anaheim Stadium to see defending champion Jeff Ward and the other great athletes. Rick Johnson roared out of the gate to a 9-second lead, but David eventually caught up with him. The rest of the race turned into one of the greatest one-on-one duels in supercross history. The huge crowd cheered wildly as the two riders fought back and forth, inching ahead of one another, trading the lead, banging handlebars all around the track. Three laps from the finish, David broke free of Rick and went on to win the race. When David crossed the finish line, he fell from his bike, exhausted: "My heart was doing 100 miles per hour," David said afterward.

THERE'S NOTHING LIKE THE THRILL OF BEING AIRBORNE, ESPECIALLY IF YOU'RE CROSSING THE FINISH LINE FIRST.

# Chapter 5
## The Obstacles

Moving motor-cycle races into stadiums and arenas for all to see was a great idea. But how is such a huge track built with all those jumps?

"It's simple," says Jerry West, laughing. Jerry is in charge of building the tracks for the supercross series. "All you have to do is cover the floor with thousands of sheets of plywood and over a quarter of a million square feet of plastic sheeting, top that with tons and tons of dirt mixed with tons of sand, then work the soil into a starting-gate area, banked turns, a section or two of whoop-de-doos, several double jumps and a triple jump, and perhaps an over-and-under bridge. Then line the course with 1,000 or more hay bales and dozens of banners and install a **starting gate** and a finish-line arch. That's it. It's simple."

Whew!

The racers use different techniques to maneuver over the various obstacles. It all begins at the starting line, where twenty riders line up a few feet behind the starting gate, which falls backward to open. Those who time themselves to reach the opening gate at the right moment and get maximum

**traction** will be out front at the start. If they leave too soon, they get caught in the gate.

**Kickers** are small jumps that are placed on straight-aways and elsewhere on the track to slow things down a bit. They're called kickers because when a motorcycle rides into one the rear wheel kicks up. Riders try to pop a wheelie just before hitting a kicker.

The most exciting parts of a supercross track are the double and triple jumps. Time can be saved by hurdling both or all three in one

leap instead of going over each jump individually. But such a feat takes plenty of skill and courage. The best riders accelerate hard into the first jump. Then while vaulting off the top of the jump, they leap up and pull the bike upward with their legs. This sends the bike even higher than it normally would go. Riders have been known to fly as high as 30 feet in the air and more than 80 feet down the track. Needless to say, landing the right way becomes rather important. Riders try to land on their rear wheel first and, preferably, on the backside of the last jump. More crashes occur from mistimed jumps than anything else.

Whoop-de-doos are also tricky to navigate. Whoops are a series of small jumps placed about 5 feet apart. The top riders clear the whoops by using either of two techniques. The first, in which the rider skims across the top of each whoop, is called the **Banzai** method. This method requires strength and timing. The second method is to treat the whoop like a double or triple jump and to clear as many whoops as possible. If all whoops cannot be cleared in a single leap, the rider must land between whoops, not on top of a whoop.

A lot of passing takes place at corners. It is best to stay on the inside and not drift too wide in a turn. Some corners are so sharp with steep banks called **berms** that a rider has to bring his motorcycle almost to a stop.

Riders also have to watch out for **ruts**. As the motorcycles go around the track, their tires dig into the dirt and create grooves. If a rider's front tire gets caught in one of these ruts, it can flip his motorcycle upside down.

Jumps, kickers, ruts, and whoop-de-doos aren't the only obstacles on the track. Riders also must contend with traffic! There are twenty competitive racers bumping elbows as they jockey for position. Who said competing in a supercross is easy?

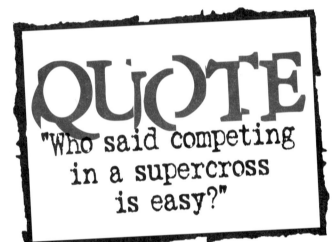

QUOTE
"Who said competing in a supercross is easy?"

IT TAKES
STRENGTH AND
TIMING TO SKIM
ACROSS WHOOP-
DE-DOOS.

27

# Chapter 6

# Practice Pays Off

Supercross beginners drive gingerly over the jumps and carefully down the straightaways. Racers with decent skills turn the throttle wide open and gun it over the jumps and down the straightaways. But the *great* riders, the ones who consistently finish in the front of the pack, are the riders who are able to combine these two styles. There's a fine line between being too careful and going full blast all the time. Finishing last is no good. Crashing is worse.

Mike Kiedrowski is a master at controlling his motorcycle. Maybe that's why he's won all three major motocross titles and now ranks among the greatest supercross riders.

"I'm more of a conservative, smooth rider," Mike says. "Not too flashy."

Mike represents Team

AGGRESSIVE RIDERS OFTEN GO TOO FAST AND CAUSE TERRIBLE CRASHES LIKE THIS.

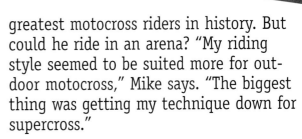

**MIKE KIEDROWSKI IS A VERY CON-TROLLED RIDER WHO CAN HANDLE STEEP TURNS AS WELL AS ANYONE.**

Kawasaki. He gets free motorcycles and equipment along with bonus money in return for wearing the company's logo on his racing outfit. Team manager Roy Turner appreciates Mike's smart style. "Mike is a very con-trolled rider. He generally doesn't take any risks and always rides within his lim-its. I think his biggest riding asset is having the ability to deal with saving himself from near crashes. He knows how to find the brakes, stop, regroup, and go on."

Mike won the AMA National Motocross Championship in the 125cc class in 1989 and 1991, in the 500cc class in 1992, and in the 250cc class in 1993. With four outdoor national titles, Mike had become one of the

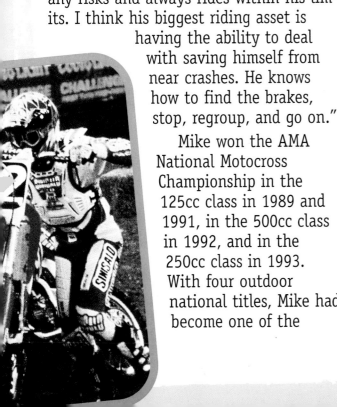

greatest motocross riders in history. But could he ride in an arena? "My riding style seemed to be suited more for out-door motocross," Mike says. "The biggest thing was getting my technique down for supercross."

Mike owns a home in Acton, California, nestled on five acres of land. He also owns several vehicles, including a Ferrari Testarossa. He used the land to build a supercross track behind his house. Now he practices supercross riding every day. And it has paid off. Mike reeled off four straight top-four-points finishes entering the 1995 AMA season. (Drivers accumulate points at each race to determine overall series finishes.) He picked up his first event victory in 1993 at the prestigious Daytona race. "It was awesome," he says. "Daytona is like the biggest supercross race of the year, so it was a real good place to get my first [win]. It would have to be the biggest single win of my career."

To prove the Daytona victory was no fluke, Mike came back a few weeks later to win the event at the Silverdome in Pontiac, Michigan.

"It takes both physical training and mental preparation to be a winner," Mike says. "I train hard because I know that if I get tired 20 minutes into the race I'm not going to win. But it's just as important to be mentally ready. For me, the mental part of it begins a couple of days prior to a race. That's when I start thinking about the track and putting everything else out of my mind."

Despite all his success, Mike is widely considered to be the nicest of racers. "I like to go with the flow. Just do my own thing and treat people as though I was talking to myself."

Since Mike has won four motocross championships and is still battling for his first supercross title, it would seem that he prefers racing outdoors. Not so.

"I like supercross better for several reasons," he says. "I like the crowds; there are usually more fans at supercross races. I like the cleanliness of the stadiums—no dust, and some of the stadiums are covered when it's raining outside. I also like the pit areas better because they're usually on concrete."

Mike will like supercross even more when he claims his first national points title.

> ## QUOTE
> "It takes both physical training and mental preparation to be a winner."

RIDERS MUST DECIDE WHEN TO PASS AND WHEN TO JUST GO WITH THE FLOW.

# CHAPTER 7

# A High School Superstar

Damon Huffman was among a group of teenagers released an hour early each day from Saugus (California) High School. The rest of the kids went off to earn minimum wage (or a little more) at their part-time jobs. Damon went off to earn thousands of dollars riding a motorcycle.

You'd think Damon would be a hero among his schoolmates in Southern California. The truth is, not many people knew where he went after school. Damon didn't like to brag.

"Only my close friends knew that I raced," Damon says, "and I guess you could say that they did all of my bragging for me."

There was plenty to brag about. Damon placed sixth in the 125cc Western Region Supercross series in his junior year, and then he won four events and finished third overall in the nation in his senior year, 1993. "I was kind of quiet about it," Damon says, "and people at my school really had no idea what level I was competing at."

Damon had the same conversation over and over again at school.

"Oh, you're on Team Suzuki," a schoolmate would say. "Does that mean you get a free bike?"

"Yes," Damon would answer shyly. "But it's more like six or seven bikes."

His schoolmates would laugh. "Yeah, right," they would say.

Damon got the same reaction when he arrived at school after winning the 125cc supercross at Anaheim Stadium. "A lot of the kids at school knew that I was going to be racing, and the next day a lot of them asked me how I did," Damon says. "When I told them that I won, they just acted like they didn't believe me. It wasn't until they started seeing me on TV that they came around."

RIDERS SUCH AS DAMON HUFFMAN FLY HIGH ON THE TRACK.

Damon had bigger concerns than convincing his schoolmates of who he was. Homework, for instance. "There were times when I just wanted to tell my parents that I wanted to drop out of school and concentrate on my racing, but I never got around to bringing it up," he says.

It was especially difficult for Damon to leave school Thursday for a weekend event, miss classes completely on Friday, return home late Sunday night, get up early Monday morning for school, and make up the class time he missed Friday.

Damon is now a high-school graduate who is thankful that he did not drop out. "I think that school is real important," he says, "but I sure am glad that I don't have to do homework on airplanes anymore."

Even though Damon's classroom studies have ended for now, he still learns some valuable lessons on the track. One such lesson came after finishing an impressive second behind Jeremy McGrath, in his heat race for the 1992 supercross event at the Los Angeles Coliseum. "I was so excited that I decided to do a **clicker** off of the finish-line jump," Damon remembers. "When I went up the face of the jump, my front wheel started to slip, and I got totally sideways in the air and crashed when I landed. I was so embarrassed! I got up and waved and bowed to the crowd and tried to play it off, but I was probably pretty red underneath my helmet."

Now Damon says when he feels like showing off after winning a race or placing high, he thinks back to his embarrassing crash at the Los Angeles Coliseum. It just confirms what he's known all along—that no matter how great you may be at something, it's better to stay humble. Safer, too.

JEREMY MCGRATH IS OFTEN OUT IN FRONT, BUT JEREMY KNOWS RIDERS LIKE DAMON HUFFMAN ARE CLOSING IN FAST.

# Chapter 8

# A Sport for the Physically Fit

A longstanding sports debate is this: What sport features the most physically fit athletes? Some say pro basketball. Some say marathon running. Some even say amateur wrestling (not to be confused with the fake pro stuff). And there are many sports fans who claim that supercross riders are the best athletes alive today.

If not, they're close to it. If so, then Jeff Stanton might be the most physically fit athlete in America. There isn't a rider today who trains harder than Jeff.

"I really admire Jeff Stanton," says Mike Bell. "His work ethic is so strong. I think that's what shines above anything else he does."

Mike should know. He was a dominant supercross champion in the 1980s who had his own intense training regimen. "As a rider," Mike says, "I think I have a different perspective from the average fan who goes to the races to see the high-flying cross-ups and whatnot. I can really appreciate the hours that go into training and all that Stanton has been able to do by working so hard at it. I really respect him for that."

Jeff has more than the respect of his peers. He also has six AMA championships—three each in 250cc supercross and 250cc motocross. And he'd like to be racing in the

twenty-first century, too.

Jeff sweats off as much as 10 or 15 pounds in a hot supercross event. But that's an easy workout compared to what he puts his body through during weekdays. "I train an average of about four hours a day, plus a couple more hours riding," Jeff says. "I ride my bicycle and run every day, and then I like to swim, ride my Jet Ski, and lift weights."

Jeff's unyielding schedule pays off. In the closing laps of races, when other riders are fading, Jeff kicks it into a higher gear. He has won more than half his races by claiming the lead in the last five laps. "I work hard at what I do," he says. "The effort you put in shows up in what you get out."

SUPERCROSS RIDERS LIKE EZRA LUSK ARE AMONG THE MOST PHYSICALLY FIT ATHLETES IN THE WORLD.

37

# Chapter 9

# Tough Competition

Steve Lamson had always done well with the lighter 125cc motorcycles on the outdoor tracks. He figured the switch to the 250cc class for supercross would be a snap. It wasn't.

"It was a lot tougher riding the heavier bike for 30 minutes straight," Steve remembers. "On top of that, the pace was just unbelievable. The first few races I was thinking, 'This is hard!'"

Steve eventually adapted to the tougher supercross events, and today he is one of the sport's elite racers. But he has plenty of competition.

Doug Henry captured two 125cc supercross championships in the early 1990s before moving up to the heavier 250cc class, in which he continues to win. "I never really cared about being the best in the world," he says, "but I guess I'm not really too far from that point now."

Jeff Emig has a flashy style that carried him to a motocross championship in 1992. He has even won international events. Now he's in pursuit of a national supercross title. "The competition had better watch out," Jeff warns.

Cliff Palmer is the only rider of a European-built motorcycle (a KTM) to consistently challenge the Japanese manufacturers. Cliff qualified for 14 main events in his 1993 rookie year, and he hasn't looked back.

Other prominent supercross competitors today include Robbie Reynard, who won his first supercross at the minimum age of sixteen; veteran Jeff Matiasevich from Anaheim Hills, California; Larry Ward from Society Hill, South Carolina; Phil Lawrence from Menifee, California; veteran Yamaha rider Mark Craig; Denny Stephenson from Omaha, Nebraska; Mike Fisher from El Cajon, California; Mexican champion Pedro Gonzalez; 1994 125cc Eastern champion Ezra Lusk; and many more.

"The competition is tougher than ever before," says champion Jeremy McGrath. "I don't know where all these good racers come from. But they just keep coming."

JEFF EMIG HAS SOARED TO INTERNATIONAL TITLES, AND HE WARNS THAT THE NATIONAL COMPETITION "HAD BETTER WATCH OUT."

# Chapter 10

# A Sport for All Seasons

The 16-race AMA Supercross series runs each year from January to June. Then what?

What else? Motocross! The AMA National series runs through September, and almost all the supercross riders make the switch to the outdoor course. Then there are the races in Europe to fill in the remaining weekends.

"I do about 56 races a year, so it doesn't make for a lot of spare time," says veteran Jeff Stanton. "Racing has taken me around the world. I wouldn't trade it for anything."

The top racers know that to stay on top they must train consistently when they aren't competing. It makes for a crammed schedule. Free time might seem precious, but most racers don't know what to do with it when they get it "Whenever I get time off and stay home, I get bored," says racer Brian Swink. "I like life on the road,

MIKE CRAIG IS AMONG THOSE FAVORED TO CAPTURE FUTURE SUPERCROSS TITLES.

trying to make things work week after week. I just love to race."

The motocross season runs thirteen weeks, until mid-September. Aside from offering more races and prize money for the motorcycle racers, there is another benefit to the motocross season—that is, a chance to redeem oneself. There's one thing worse than suffering through a poor supercross season. That's thinking about it. If motocross competition didn't exist, a

MEXICAN NATIONAL CHAMPION PEDRO GONZALEZ IS LEAVING HIS MARK TODAY IN STADIUMS THROUGHOUT THE UNITED STATES.

racer might have to dwell on his miserable season from June until the following January. Motocross is a good escape. And sometimes even more.

The 1992 AMA Supercross season looked bright for veteran Mike LaRocco when he won the series opener in Orlando, Florida. But disaster struck two weeks later when Mike fell in a practice run. He suffered a broken wrist and was knocked from the supercross competition. All he could do was rehabilitate his wrist and wait for the motocross season. It gave him something to look forward to.

Although Mike missed the first event of the eight-week 250cc

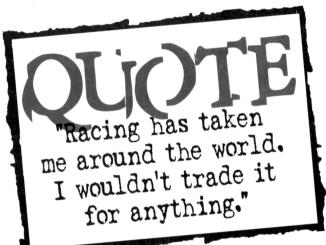

QUOTE

"Racing has taken me around the world. I wouldn't trade it for anything."

motocross series, he came on strong and finished second overall in points. More determined than ever, Mike roared through the month-long 500cc series to cap the year with his first national championship of any kind. What started as a terrible supercross season ended as Mike's most memorable racing year ever.

"Winning the 500cc title was a necessity," Mike says with a smile.

It's easy to smile after you win. But supercross riders seem to smile no matter what. In the first 25 years of the sport, fewer than 50 different racers have won a main event. But thousands have competed—and smiled. You would too if you got to ride a motorcycle for a living.

GRITTY MIKE LAROCCO OVERCAME A BROKEN WRIST TO CAPTURE HIS FIRST NATIONAL CHAMPIONSHIP.

43

# GLOSSARY

**Banzai** A term that describes a method used by riders to skim across a series of bumps

**berm** A steep turn banked to the inside of the track

**BMX bikes** A bicycle used primarily by children for racing

**cc** Abbreviation for "cubic centimeters," in which engine size is measured

**clicker** A showy trick that a rider performs during a jump

**circuit** The schedule of events in a supercross season

**hairpin turn** An extremely sharp turn on a track

**heat race** A preliminary race held to eliminate some contenders

**kickers** Small jumps placed throughout the track to momentarily slow the riders

**motocross (MX)** Motorcycle racing performed outdoors across natural terrain

**rut**  A small but dangerous groove created by tires digging into the dirt

**starting gate**  A metal gate that falls backward to allow riders to start the race

**straightaway**  A straight stretch of track

**supercross**  Motorcycle racing performed on a track in a stadium or an arena

**throttle**  The right handgrip, or accelerator, which controls the power of the motorcycle

**traction**  The ability of tires to grip the dirt surface without slipping

**whoop-de-doo**  A rippling series of high bumps placed about 5 feet apart

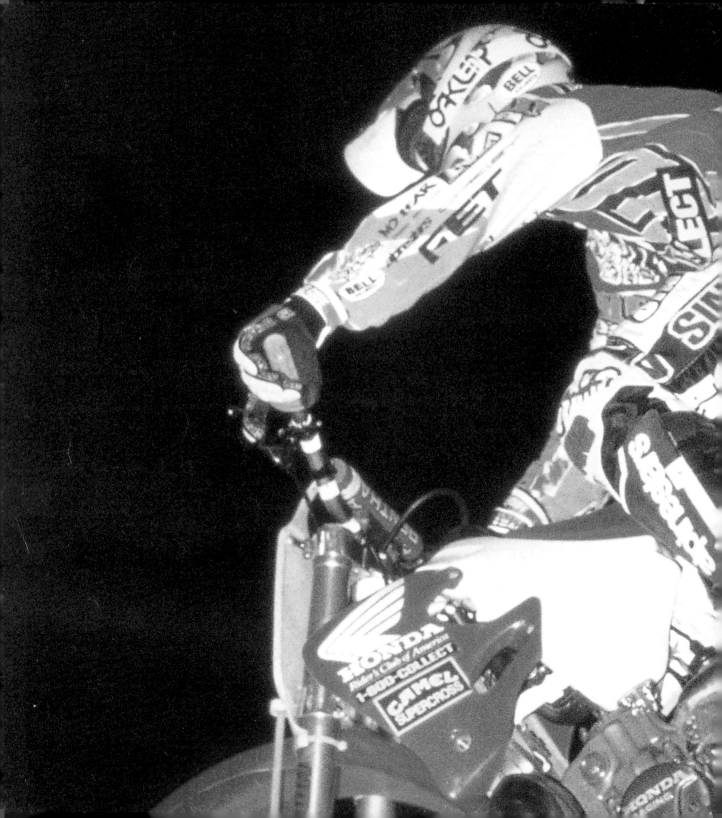

# INDEX